Goodbye, Oyster Girls

Melanie McClellan-Hartnett

Goodbye, Oyster Girls

Melanie McClellan-Hartnett

BROAD
RIVER
BOOKS

GOODBYE OYSTER, GIRLS. Copyright 2018 by Melanie McClellan-Hartnett.

All rights reserved. Printed in Columbia, South Carolina in the United States of America. No part of this book may be used or reproduced in any manner whatsoever without written permission except in the case of brief quotations embodied in critical articles and reviews.

Broad River Books
is an imprint of
MuddyFordPress.com

Library of Congress Number: 2018967543
ISBN: 978-1-942081-19-7

Cover Art by Tommy Beaver

For Joseph and Chloë,
who bring their mom more joy than they can possibly know
and
Robert,
who holds my heart

Contents

Introduction   9
Conversation   11
Pearl   12
Driftwood   13
You Are the Sea   14
Valentine   15
To Unborn Chloë   16
Dryad   17
Tonight On the Deck   18
Lowcountry   19
Hurricane Hugo   21
Penelope   22
Antigone   23
Good Save   24
After I Threw Hay to the Horses   25
Among the Things I Wish This Morning   26
Marsh Daughter   27
Question   29
Silence   30
For Joseph Whose Smile is the Wider for Missing Teeth   31
You Stood   32
Toast   33
Helen   34
Oyster Girls   35
Lilypads   36
Beautiful   37
Flag Stones   38
Marsh Voices   39
Marooned   42

January Thin Sunshine   43
Fledglings   44
Past War   45
Haunted   46
Penelope Again   47
Psyche   48
Chameleon So Invisible   49
Drift   50
Another Way   51
What the Housewife Saw   52
Mad Women of the Marshes   53
White Bells of Mallows   57
Miami Playa   58
Soon   59
A Possible Bridge   60
Lady of Shallot   61
Tides' Tale   63
Phoenix   66
Marsh Lament   67
Homecoming   68
If a Transparent Moth   69
Acknowledgements   70

Introduction

If it were left up to her, you'd be reading this long after Melanie McClellan-Hartnett had gone. It'd be about 2080, and this book would be a tattered layering of frayed pages on a picked-over table at a rummage sale. This poet isn't looking for recognition. She's looking for connection, no matter the time and place. And she's trying to get these poems out of her head.

Melanie is nothing if not a creative thinker. As a child, her solution to her family's financial problems was to excavate moon rocks and sell them. As an adult, she works for a slim stipend, bringing an art program she designed to the very young and very old —and often very poor—in her beloved McClellanville. It's her way of healing her universe, this salty-sweet, languid-violent, sometimes too closely knit enclave of villagers, many of them her kin. She pays them homage in this collection of poems, many of which were praised by her College of Charleston English professors.

Some might think this poet hasn't ventured far from the marshes of her South Carolina home. *Au contraire.* Melanie has lived in England, Costa Rica, and Mexico, and explored the American West and Spain. Her experiences of other cultures give her the authority to describe the desultory action/inaction of the people on the porches in "Lowcountry."

What people clutch and display says a lot about who they are. It might confound some that Melanie won two prizes from the South Carolina Poetry Society years ago but misplaced the documentation congratulating her for her achievement. She was too busy – raising two children with her husband Robert, advocating for a clean environment, working with others to transform her SmashGlass art program into the Smashing Barriers movement, which has brought people of all incomes, ages, and races together. All this while working through the crises and upheaval bipolar disorder wreaks.

Goodbye, Oyster Girls reflects the poet's battles and loves, her hopes for a fairer South, and her observations of nature and people. Part mermaidish Ophelia— "Marsh Daughter," "Mad Woman of the Marshes"—part wood nymph, "Dryad," Melanie McClellan-Hartnett puts her worlds of imagination and reality into her wise art. Three things tell you all you need to know about her: 1) Robert knew her engagement ring needed to be a pearl, not a diamond; 2) their annual Summer Solstice party always includes a maypole dance; and 3) her greatest wish for this book is to be able to give a copy to her grandmother.

Aïda Rogers

July 2018
McClellanville, SC

Conversation

Arched and trembling
The wave curls.
My mother said,
I do not understand
These Village girls.

Pearl

She has listened to the waters
So long songs have ceased
Circling
Rhythm of reeds
Unfolding
Into a great
Stillness
Clear as glass.
It is the making
Of a pearl.

O Southern Sons
Thank your God.

Oysters blooming in the mud
Oysters blooming in the mud

Driftwood

lost SeWee lost Gullah lost Geechee lost
goodbye oyster girls
luminous bygone pearls
slipped through grasping hands
lie latent in the sands
lost

she charts unwritten connections—
tributaries of
blood—bone—spittle—semen—flesh
known backwaters—
forgotten creeks—of
dreams—sorrows—cruelties—sacrifice—vengeance—
words spoken—
passing from one
to another—to another—to another—
losing
form and particulars—
shells softened
in waves—
stones smoothed in the
salt water—
ebenezers of hope—
remnants of a lost faith
shaken out of children's pockets in the wash

a woman holds them in her
shaking hand
reminded
of something
she hears in her
dreams
she reads the song of the reeds in her native tongue.

You Are the Sea

All rivers run to your ocean.
I am the breakers
Ceaseless change crashing
On the same shore.

I remember you
Across the years
I see your face
Feel the home of your embrace
Face pressed to your chest
I have timed my breathing
To your heart
Have found myself spent
After a storm
And the sun was
Your eyes and
The sea was your arms

Valentine

Persian rug in Persian blue
Red knickers
Fallen to the floor
In the attitude of a
Heart

To Unborn Chloe

Sitting in the faded grass field one
Hand where your growing form
Swells mine into a wave trembling
With the motion of your living
Watching the birds migrating across
The blue white sky ceiling
Understanding how the earth
Endures bleak winter serenely
With all the songs and flowers
Of the world
Inside her womb

Dryad

Trees—you O dryad
Know the feel
Of their skin
The rhythms
Of their leaves
The deep earth drinking song
Of stars
You climb them all
Climbing outside
Yourself
Leaving
Your body propped
In the curve of limbs
Wandering time and space
Gazing upon eternity
Breathing the greenness
You come into the house
And you smell of
Live oaks water oaks white oaks
Tupelo cedar bay holly hickory
Dogwood sweet gum myrtle
Fennel wind
Sun moon
Rain earth
Living
glowing
soul
You
The trees
Call
By name

Tonight On The Deck

In a purple paisley kimono
You flapped your arms to be a moth
And your right hand hit a weathered spindle
Just exactly like a moth.
You did not cry
But folded yourself against
The redwood chaise and said
You were a moth with a broken wing

Lowcountry

spun of porches—
hammocks—
sun dapples—
inconstant clinking of ice cubes melting—
dwindling icebergs diluting
the inevitably sweet tea.
evenings people lay in hammocks
on the screened porch
listening to cicadas—
watching heat lightning
murmuring friends stopping over—
consuming gallons of iced tea—
sprawling over the porch
pajama-clad children
floating like moths past the screens—
shrilling through the dewfall—
chasing fireflies.

birdchirpy languorous peachvelvet afternoons
heart grown too still—
summer too hot—
stagnant—
putting all to sleep in hammocks on porches.
The Lowcountry becomes one strung-out eternal party—
Flimsy flammable thing
the sight of whose garish trinkets
Gaudy dazzle
Hung-over eyes
Everyone has a mint julep—high ball—margarita
To meet the unbearable sight
of our neighbors ever again after last night
and the night before.

Civilization gone to seed.
Heat too oppressive—
dreams too scorching—
Everyone secretly prays for a hurricane
washing over languid hands with Neptune's mighty ocean
A hurricane party is the best kind of party
So long as the liquor holds

A town of drunks and stoners
And leave-me-aloners
Former slave owners…

It was a porch of despair
The way they slumped in their chairs
Faces stymied stares
From which no prospect
Was visible

Hurricane Hugo

Was the Flood
Buried dolphins in the mud
Driftwood rabble
Now it's Babel

Penelope

Everyday I am Penelope
Weaving my tapestry
A picture begins to formulate
Daily patterns
Love and hate
Stacked between
The sink and plates
Almost I glimpse a story
Nightly unraveled
Fraying ever more apart—
The seas you have traveled
To the chamber of my heart

Antigone

Rejoice O Mother
For answered prayers
Though raped—despoiled
And robbed of heirs

Land soaked with blood
Of murdered seeds,
Long have you withstood
Your men's misdeeds

Mother America
Sea to shining sea
Queen or quarry
As needs may be

The end justifies the means
Victor sleeps with the Queen
Might makes right
They got the pistols
They get the pesos
Capiche?

No.

Mother, show me what you see
That your heart does not die of grief
Manifest Destiny—unclear to me—
Help Thou mine unbelief.

Silent faith of your Love
Beneath scars you don't deserve
Wordless serenity unmoved

Good Save

Good thing I can use a word
Turned expertly as a sword
Or that sentence we just heard
Might settle smutty hand above my knee

And then where would we be?
It's damn awkward.
And do I want
The f----- Trojan war?

If a girl can fight her own fight
Why unleash the warrior might
Of the injured husband's right?

Imagine the
Consequences

After I Threw Hay to the Horses

I opened the screened porch
Door and felt my hair all
Autumn cold against my ears
And saw the jack-o-lanterns
On the table

Among the Many Things I Wish This Morning

Is the hope that the mocking bird
In the dogwood tree with red berries
Will stop attacking his reflection
In the window

Marsh Daughter

Rings on rings in the water
my hand trailing in the water
over the edge of a boat
marking a white trail over the water
skiff shifting across the glassy surface
the wake furrowing out
splashes on the marsh the salt water
splashing over
the pluff mud and oysters
echoes back
a child's hand trailing in the water
they know me
they know my children
and it sounds like madness
it sounds so like madness.
I cannot swear
that it is not mad
only that it is true
and these are not mutually exclusive
they are there
I can feel them
hear them and almost see them but
they are always shimmering just out of reach
murmuring shadows wavelets against the shellbank beach
fluttering hieroglyphics of something
I should plainly know
We all dream briny lapping
wash up stranded
and awake
against the bosom of a mother
daily battered
o mother of sorrows
ceaselessly weeping

Rachel weeping for her sons
o God do not all mothers weep
for their sons and their daughters
holding only to the faith that is love?
aren't we all haunted tainted taunted?
some shadows
lie deep.

spirits
yes
spirits

Spirits
That would be bourbon, right?
There's some as
It's no good speaking spirits.
Let it rest.
Breathe.

I'll time my breathing
To the creek.
It flows east
Seaward
Ever
Would I go
Where all the waters of the world
Even out in a sheen
Outstretching the farthest archipelagoes
Of reed and bank
Into endlessly
Ascending
Light

Question

She looked hard at him.
She said, "Sometimes it feels like you ask trick questions."
He laughed.
"Sometimes it feels like you give trick answers."
She looked hard at him.
"Oh," she said, "that isn't fair. I don't try.
An answer follows a question.
You ask such hard questions!"
He laughed again.
"'Do you want to go to sleep?' is a hard question?"
"Yes."

Silence

Loudest silence still unbroken
Latent weight of words not spoken
We're not much
For conversation
Tonight

For Joseph Whose Smile is the Wider for Missing Teeth

Between missing bits
In your baby
Gapped smile
I see the sunsets
Mile on mile

So very you.

So much so
Your light fills
The emptiness

You Stood

Against the sky
Framed in the doorway
Caged by bars of
Kitchenlight—
Arching your arms
Against approaching night
Shoulders writhing as if
You could cast aside
Mortality
Howling
At the moon
Framed in the doorway
Shivering shadow in gray pajamas
Chest taut
Breathing
Free

Toast

To the fair destroyer
The daughter of the South
To Helen
Whose protean eyes
And treacherous dimple
Do first herself destroy
In full view
Of knights and squires
Still gathering to die
On her perilous
Quest

Helen

My sultry beauty—
Swaying hips
Awakes their duty—
Launches ships
Ten years war
Because I'm impure?
Are they false or fools?
I am not sure

Could they seek themselves to cleanse?
In their hearts force of desire—
In their loins carnal fire—
But screwing whores
Are holy sins

Lauding their law
Applauding power that they wield
The ends justifies the means
Brutality to combat depravity
A Cause to fight—
The perfect shield

They must be lofty indeed
Who make the weak to bleed

If a man succumb to lust
The woman is to blame
Rape and trample in the dust
Burn bright o sacred flame

Oyster Girls

At Maybank Hall
Blood between the bricks
Seeping over patrons' names
Bloodfire sun
Licks the columns
Occasions solemn
Cancer sticks and parlor tricks
Ashes of Atlanta's flames
Descending Belles
Carefully freakishly bred
Cultured amongst the dead
Ancestors- ghosts- curses
Lily white hands
Bloodstained lands
Gnashing swine
Grinding pearls
Oddly luminous
Oyster girls

Lilypads

Red my underside as blood spilled
Scarlet ribbed cut beef
Waving, crimson, thick-veined hand
Sultry, weary, gently lifted fan
Held by the jaded geisha
I lift; waver, fall
Love, it is this still pond, this quiet water
Smothered beneath pure white lilies
Languid homage, shifting in the wind
Green ruffles across the water
Womankind, the world's great harem
But here is no cause
No cause to fret
Sheiks war, conquer, trade frantic
Perpetual motion
My roots never leave this stagnant pool
Grow tannic with the water
Wind will not penetrate
These shallow depths

Beautiful

People say she was beautiful
They still say she is rich
Cracked out squatter
When she speaks you hear
How far away she is.
Her voice echoes through the legions
Her mind has wandered.
Her words lurch into the moment
Like a hand coming down too hard on a table.
She waves her hands.
She says
"Aren't you beautiful? Beautiful.
God bless you angels."

Flag Stones

Looking at the flags
We are accumulating one
Paycheck at a time to fill
In the sand at the
Foot of the stairs
I think of this house and
These flags in one hundred years
And I remember
What Stuart Macintosh's father
Told him
And what prompted him
To find the meteorite now
In the Village Museum
"There are no rocks around
Here. You see a rock,
Somebody brought it
From somewhere else."

Marsh Voices

It begins in the blood
seeping through mud
oozing through thoughts
water through salt
and you know it is madness
you know it must be madness
you know
it will not go away

what is it that remains incarnate
slowly eroding into itself again?
crust forming on the marsh grasses
feel it stir as it passes
one touch
sets off a vibrating chain
linking one lifetime to another
so many myriad links
growing encasing swelling erasing
Linking me to the Ancients
I fetch up on a distant shore
and recognize in the contour of its arm that of my sister
yes sister for it is she
mother daughter it could be
lying there prone
yes prone
oh dead and gone

some say dead and gone

this is not so
blood does not go
the ones that weep
the ones that bleed

have sown these fields immortal seed
and yes I wash up on the shore
and find her my sister

she whispers
they all whisper through her
every woman in the reeds
every woman weeps
every woman bleeds
rings on rings in the water
moon and tides
mother daughter

it sounds like madness
I know it cannot be said
and unsaid again
we cannot pretend
I cannot pretend now
because I know
they are there
I cannot say how

I know they are linked
We are all linked
rings on rings in the water
moon and tides
mother daughter
sister aunt cousin friend
weeping bleeding all together
imprints congregate
magnetic throbbing growing
plankton life form weaving
calling

come to us come to us
if you fear if you need
if you sob if you bleed

Hear them calling
Hear them
Ghosts in the marsh

over water
echoes throbbing
Vibrating through
the pulsing song
Of my inhabited shell

Marooned

The sound of tears
A constant
Dripping
Finally
Every room flooded
A corner of the roof
Your only
Escape

January Thin Sunshine

I tried to stand in the rays
Always shifting
Light and shadows playing
Across your face

Fledglings

Now you begin your flight
Moving with speed
And power given
Solely to you
Wings to wend
Where you will

Soaring at last
As you were born to do
Reveling in the glory
Of youth

It makes my heart
Sing
To see
You

Free against sky and tree
Small in eternity
Potently
Individually
Alive

A light
Emanating from your heart
Alone
A star
In the universe
Shining

Past War

Leaves a scar
Man willed
Blood spilled
There is no before
No "if not for the War"
No innocents that we were
Only the people we are
Defaced and deformed
Debased and informed
Naked
With the knowledge
Of death

Haunted

Constant voices in my head
Narrating scenes I have not seen
Voices- neither alive nor dead—
Come from somewhere in between
What has been
Will be again

Penelope Again

I am weary of your quests
All the things necessary
To your universe
All for my ultimate good
"Loved I not honor more"
Is no light gift
I'm sure

I could invite my own guests
And adlib the rest
I could beat my breast
But no more.
You have never understood
"no more"
You take a lot for granted
When you come ashore.

Psyche

Ragged Psyche naked raving
Doesn't know she needs saving
Castle all in ruins
This is not Cupid's doing

Chameleon So Invisible

I am surprised by
Your transparent face
I have never been sure.
It has always been
Your one magician's trick:
Love-
Dazzling carnival bizarre
Casts me spinning through
Light and shadow
Onto a shore of grace.

Drift

We break away
Continents splitting
Friends and customs
Divided
Fissured
Drift beyond bridging

Your face grows
Smaller
Every
day

Another Way

There is another way
To erase this woman
And that is to take away
All that she loves—
Not that way
Not that way
Not that way
God, I pray
Keep them safe—
Let them stay

What the Housewife Saw

Morning

The water is still clear
In the dented wash tub but there was
That lizard—drowned---
The way her body drooped
Across the stick that fished her out
The way she hung
Without resistance
Without ever again the chance
To meet a male anole with his heart in his throat.

Afternoon

It is hard to see how it could be so easily missed
That the belted kingfisher darting
Past the autumn russet cypress
Is the same song
As the red gold cypress and the sharp sky

Mad Woman of the Marshes

Earth song in my blood
I cannot alter this
Throbbing in pluff mud
Pulsing through my pores
After earth returns to earth
There is something more
Water will return to water
Still the song endures
The song teems in blood and water
Contracts- expands through air
The song is in the spirit
The spirit is everywhere

Hush you shall not say
You know of spirits
That's crazy talking, sister
They'll put you away
You crazy, you got
No rights

You call this crazy?
I'll show you
Crazy
Crazy is this song
Bursting through--
Torment constantly heard--
Crazy-- this torrent
Years of pent up words
Crazy is the stopping of my ears
To the song some do not hear
And do not understand
And fear
Crazy for me to deny

The song is here
After earth returns to earth
There is something more
Water will return to water
Still the song endures
I cannot alter this
Song a rising tide
Humming in my blood
Throbbing through my heart
Flooding capillaries
Creeks running over
Sky sheen reflection
Pierced by blades of grass
Soft percussion of waves
Salt wind whispers of the past
The song is in the spirit
The spirit is everywhere
I cannot alter this
You talk of crazy
It's crazy talk
To halt a tide

Whole damn world crazy
But you
You're certified
You're in their books
Sister, they decide
You too crazy
They shut you up
Everybody and his brother
Know better than you, crazy
You got no rights
Push comes to shove

If it comes to that
We all know where it's at
They got the pistols
They get the pesos
Is Justice blind that never saw
How enforcers of the law
Call all the shots?
Their word over yours
His word over hers
The girl is always much to blame
I need not explain this drill
There's not a woman born
Who doesn't know
Might makes right
This game's not new
Crazy got no rights?
Sister, you
Got that right
And neither do you
Push come to shove
But
I will not despair
The hope I cannot see
I know that they are there
Though I cannot translate the words
Of the song they sing
I will follow the chords
Through my heart's labyrinth
Feet bare in wave lapped water
Sticky with oozing mud
Salt and cedar on the wind
I will not fear
Spirits whispering
Of places hidden
Forces bidden

Interlacing creeks —solitary—entwined
The secret paths
Beyond the maps
I am of this place
Native daughter
My blood runs thick
With the song of these spirits
Song of tide and moon and women
Rise fall wax wane bloom wither
Again again again
All the women who came before us
Wept and bled and sang the chorus
Lived—sang--
Sing still
Song
Echoing
Expanding rings
Across the water
Against the shore
Invisible now
Trembling through atoms
Of quicksand mud
Whispered between reeds
Breathed in humid vapor
Returning to the sky
After earth returns to earth
There is something more
Water will return to water
Still the song endures
The earth will always triumph
Body battered children scattered beauty shattered
In the end these do not matter
She will begin again
She holds against the heartache
Her womb filled with springs

White Bells of Mallows

Under tree shadows
Creeks of black water
Running hidden
Running incessant
Running through my hands
Pressed between
Your hands
Every grain of sand
Beneath me—singing
Above-- wind through trees
Clouds and sky
Too pale for blue

Miami Playa

Oleanders line the street
Where palm and orange trees meet
Red tiled roofs—whitewashed walls—
On the beach the peddlers call
Sky blue water—sun-bleached sand—
Dark tanned lovers hand in hand
Salty children in the water
Almost grown son and daughter

Soon

You will fly away
As you were born to do
I always knew you would
Someday
The last cord that holds you
Hangs by a thread

A Possible Bridge

Egrets used to be there
In that bend in the bridge—
The first bridge—the old one with
Monstrous iron lashings and
Rusting bolts— narrow
Crooked spine across the Harbor
That was hell to drive.
Divers could swim through holes in the
Base of the structure, people said.
They built a better bridge
But the egrets had already flown
Leaving Drum Island
Leaving us
Alone
With the hollow beating of waves
And dreams of a possible bridge
To span the divide
That sent them so far away

Lady of Shalott

Things I see in the mirror
Fill me with terror—
Staring out at me—insane
Inescapable
Destiny
Only just kept at bay
Pray I am capable
Pray I am capable
Pray pray pray

Can I trust this looking glass?
Always weaving the future—
Letting the moment pass.
Caged in this room
With shuttle and loom
My song escapes the window—
My body heavy in this room
Waiting for doom
Waiting for doom
It is coming soon

I saw him coming ere I saw him
Knowing he was going
Where I may never see
Accursed if I look in his direction—
If I see more than this reflection
It is the end of me

Collect myself
Inspect myself
Protect myself

Dear God these voices in my head!
Would they be silenced if I were dead?

I need not see him with my eyes
The truth within the mirror lies
….How like an angel is this devil
How bright his armor's shone
That one so fair could be so evil…
I cannot bear the sight
Of this treacherous lecherous knight
He'll break the heart and ring
Of his best friend the king
Leaving the shamed queen exiled—
Alone

O bright fallen star
Winding down the road
To your lost mistress
How hellishly beautiful
You are

I will see this marvel
With my own eyes
And leave off spinning
My fate within me lies!

Was it worth it?
End coming just after the start?
So soon the trees block out the view
I feel my life threads snapping
Tapestry unraveling
Of course the curse holds true
Shards of mirror
Flying apart—flashing past
Shattered pieces of silvered glass
And something else
That was
My heart

Tides' Tale

The women that were--
Cried with arms extended
if you falter we will guide you
we will hide you we know the paths
lying hidden and what forces may be bidden
come to us come to us
At the lighthouse
It was
Years and years
Before I was born

Maybe tides told the story
Surely no human told me
Before I dreamed

I saw her pass him on the stairs
I felt the fear lift her breast
He let her squeeze by
But he pressed
she breathed deep sea salt air
it cried to her it called her
from the marrow of her bones
from the blood within her
called her
Daughter, sister, come to us
come to us come to us we will guide you
we will hide you we know the paths
that lay hidden and what forces may be bidden
come to us come to us
I saw them stretching out their hands
She saw too but she was afraid,
 She heard them. yes
she thought she did

after she fled him.
breathing hard against the fringe of land
gasping confronted by the creek
she was afraid.
Too long had she wept and bled
Unaided in these waters.
Fearing cursing the marsh
She turned back

The Cape Romain Lighthouse keeper
Murdered his faithless homesick wife--
Pining for her native fjords
On his deathbed he heard her in the waves
confessed for fear of his wife and her fey sisters.
legend says she brought a treasure
never found--
a trinket box of small treasures
from her other life
with her first husband
in Norway.

In my dream I saw the casket.
On her way back
When she pretended she could placate
When she pretended she could hope.
I saw her press it to her heart.
I saw her cast about
in the shrubs close by the house--
too close by.
There was water;
it must have called her.
she was running out of time.
she knew it was all too late
she would not let him take it
she flung it away.

she heard them
be brave for have you not bled here many times before?
Blood and moon and tides rushing in
and then
I saw no more

Phoenix

Can these bones live?
Lord, you know.
Prophesy to these bones:
There is only one thing
I know to prophesize:
Tendons writhing
Atoms spinning
Soul threads casting
A body so frail
You are a danger to yourself-

Rise

Marsh Lament

The Old Man of the Sea
Has turned away from me
He followed the tide
To eternity

Marsh winds whisper through the grass
I heard them sing
His funeral mass
They paid him homage in the brine
We saw egrets waiting in a line—
Six sentinels on each side
Flanked the house where he had died
Waited the turning of the tide

How shall we mourn?

We find ourselves in naked cadence
Our faces are torn
Out pasted things
Stuck about the room
With vases of luscious flowers
That do not smell of spring

Homecoming

Back to the saltwater bring his ashes
Back to the Ancients
He returns
At peace

His slow smile spreading across the water
Settling in the creek
Pulsing with the tide.

If a Transparent Moth

Flies into a clear window
Can you see anything break?
Everybody's a risk.

Acknowledgments

It is not possible to list each person in this village who raised me and whose insight, guidance, time and support are woven into the DNA of these poems. Thank you, McClellanville.

And for growing this collection into a real live book, special thanks to

>Nan Morrison and Marsha Purvis, for slogging mental marshes gamely (aka reading and culling years of poetry)

>Cindi Boiter, for giving *Oyster Girls* and so many others in South Carolina a voice

>Aïda Rogers, first, because she is a pearl and second because without her advocacy, perseverance, brains and innate ability to discern patterns in the circles on the water, this book never would have happened

>Tommy Beaver for sharing his beautiful painting

>The Creator of saltwater and all its children, for the poetry that is life

Soli Deo Gloria.

About the Author

Melanie McClellan-Hartnett grew up and still lives in McClellanville, South Carolina, where there is definitely something in the water.

She hopes any attention drawn to McClellanville via these poems will unite people in protecting the waters of this community, both private wells and shared wetlands, marshes, creeks and ocean—forging a link with the earth and those who have returned to its dust that heals, strengthens and renews the spirit of the people.

At 19, she was awarded two prizes by the Poetry Society of South Carolina. Otherwise her literary life had lain latent.

This is her first book.

www.ingramcontent.com/pod-product-compliance
Lightning Source LLC
Chambersburg PA
CBHW052206110526
44591CB00012B/2106